**W9-DBE-817**

NOTE TO PARENTS

Learning to read is an important skill for all children. It is a big milestone that you can help your child reach. The American Museum of Natural History Easy Reader program is designed to support you and your child through this process. Developed by reading specialists, each book in the series includes carefully selected words and sentence structures to help children advance from beginner to intermediate to proficient readers.

Here are some tips to keep in mind as you read these books with your child:

First, preview the book together. Read the title. Then look at the cover. Ask your child, "What is happening on the cover? What do you think this book is about?"

Next, skim through the pages of the book and look at the illustrations. This will help your child use the illustrations to understand the story.

Then encourage your child to read. If he or she stumbles over words, try some of these strategies:

- **use the pictures as clues**
- **point out words that are repeated**
- **sound out difficult words**
- **break up bigger words into smaller chunks**
- **use the context to lend meaning**

Finally, find out if your child understands what he or she is reading. After you have finished reading, ask, "What happened in this book?"

Above all, understand that each child learns to read at a different rate. Make sure to praise your young reader and provide encouragement along the way!

Introduce Your Child to Reading
Simple words and simple sentences encourage beginning readers to sound out words.

Your Child Starts to Read
Slightly more difficult words in simple sentences help new readers build confidence.

Your Child Reads with Help
More complex words and sentences and longer text lengths help young readers reach reading proficiency.

Your Child Reads Alone
Practicing difficult words and sentences brings independent readers to the next level: reading chapter books.

To editor Alli Brydon, with appreciation

—T.F.

Photo credits
Cover/jacket: © Mark Kostich/iStockphoto.com
Pages 4–5: © Tim Laman/National Geographic Stock; 6: © Chanyut Sribua-rawd/iStockphoto.com;
7 (left): © James R. D. Scott/Flickr/Getty Images; 7 (right): © M. Watson/ardea.com;
8–9: © Michael D. Kern/naturepl.com; 10–11: © Rusty Dodson/shutterstock; 12–13: © Bernhard Richter/iStockphoto.com;
14 (top): © Kim Taylor/naturepl.com; 14 (bottom): © Kim Taylor/naturepl.com; 15 (top): © Kim Taylor/naturepl.com;
15 (bottom): © Kim Taylor/naturepl.com; 16–17: © Mary McDonald/naturepl.com;
18: © Mattias Klum/National Geographic/Getty Images; 19: © Michael Richards/John Downer Productions/naturepl.com;
20–21: © Michael & Patricia Fogden/Minden Pictures; 22–23: © Dbaleckaitis/Dreamstime.com;
24: © Michael & Patricia Fogden/Corbis; 25: © Daniel Heuclin/naturepl.com;
26–27: © Michael & Patricia Fogden/Minden Pictures; 28–29: © Jim Merli/Visuals Unlimited, Inc.;
30–31: © Joseph T. Collins/Photo Researchers, Inc.
32: © Joy Nikolopoulos

STERLING CHILDREN'S BOOKS
New York

An Imprint of Sterling Publishing
387 Park Avenue South
New York, NY 10016

STERLING CHILDREN'S BOOKS and the distinctive Sterling Children's Books logo
are trademarks of Sterling Publishing Co., Inc.

© 2012 by Sterling Publishing Co., Inc., and
The American Museum of Natural History

All rights reserved. No part of this publication may be reproduced, stored in a retrieval system,
or transmitted, in any form or by any means, electronic, mechanical, photocopying, recording,
or otherwise, without prior written permission from the publisher.

ISBN 978-1-4027-9114-7 (hardcover)
ISBN 978-1-4027-7788-2 (paperback)

Distributed in Canada by Sterling Publishing
c/o Canadian Manda Group, 165 Dufferin Street
Toronto, Ontario, Canada M6K 3H6
Distributed in the United Kingdom by GMC Distribution Services
Castle Place, 166 High Street, Lewes, East Sussex, England BN7 1XU
Distributed in Australia by Capricorn Link (Australia) Pty. Ltd.
P.O. Box 704, Windsor, NSW 2756, Australia

For information about custom editions, special sales, and premium and corporate purchases,
please contact Sterling Special Sales at 800-805-5489 or specialsales@sterlingpublishing.com.

Printed in China
Lot #:
2 4 6 8 10 9 7 5 3
10/12

www.sterlingpublishing.com/kids

FREE ACTIVITIES & PUZZLES ONLINE AT
http://www.sterlingpublishing.com/kids/sterlingeventkits

AMERICAN MUSEUM
OF NATURAL HISTORY

EASY READERS

SNAKES
UP CLOSE!

Thea Feldman

STERLING CHILDREN'S BOOKS
New York

Look at this Paradise Tree Snake!

It pushed itself off a tree branch.

It makes its body flat and flies in

the air.

R0440195441

The snake will land on another tree.

Let's see some other super snakes up close.

How do snakes move?

Some snakes climb trees.

Some snakes swim.

Some snakes crawl along the ground.

SEA KRAIT

SIDEWINDER

The Sea Krait lives in the water.

It paddles forward with its tail.

The Sidewinder moves sideways on

sand to get where it needs to go.

Flick!

All snakes have forked tongues.

A snake uses its tongue to smell.

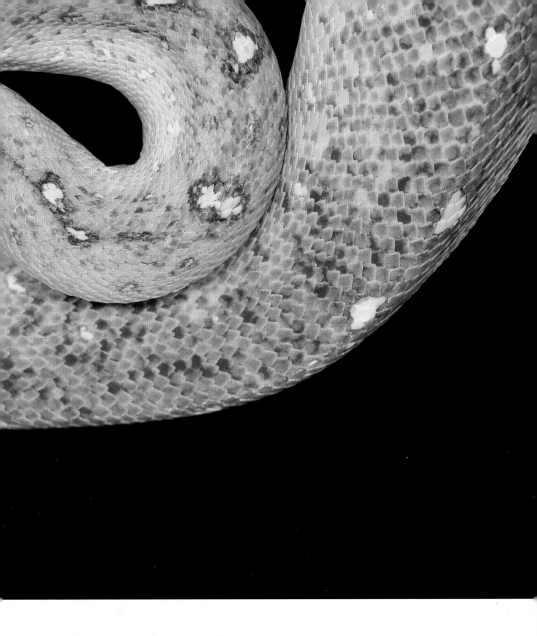

This snake sticks out its tongue.

Then it pulls it back into its mouth.

That is how it can smell a meal.

The Coachwhip lives on the ground.

It is busy during the day.

Most snakes that are busy
during the day have eyes with
big, round centers.

Rattlesnakes are busy at night.

Most snakes that are busy at night

have eyes with thin slits in the center.

nostril

heat
pit

Rattlesnakes have holes in their faces called heat pits.

Heat pits help it find animals in the dark to eat.

Gulp!

All snakes swallow their food whole.
Some snakes can open their mouths
very wide.

This lets a snake swallow something much bigger than its head.

Look at this Egg Eating Snake as it swallows an egg.

The Garden Tree Boa winds around
an animal.

It tightens its hold until the animal
cannot breathe.

Then it opens its jaws wide
and swallows the whole thing.
Snakes that do this are called
"constrictors."

The King Cobra strikes!

It bites down on an animal.

Venom passes through its sharp fangs.

The venom kills the animal.

The Spitting Cobra can spit venom
into an animal's eyes!
Snakes use venom to hunt for food
or to stay safe.

The Hognose Snake rolls over and plays dead when it senses danger.

It can also give off a bad smell.

This smell makes an enemy think

the Hognose Snake is not good to eat.

Most snakes live alone.

Some snakes live in groups when
it gets cold.

Look at all these Garter Snakes!

They will live alone when summer
is here.

Some snakes lay eggs.

The Coral Snake lays eggs

in a safe place.

Then she leaves.

The Grass Snake lays her eggs

in a warm place.

Her babies hatch on their own.

Some snakes give birth to live young.

This Pit Viper is having a baby.

Her baby will be ready to slide away.

This Kingsnake is shedding its skin!

A snake keeps growing for its whole life.

It sheds every time it gets too big

for its skin.

The snake loosens its outside
coat of skin.

Then it slides forward.

The old skin comes off in one piece.

The Tentacled Snake lives in water.

The tentacles on its face are feelers.

They feel when a fish is near.

Then the snake grabs the fish to eat.

Snakes are super!

Which one do you like best?

MEET THE EXPERT!

My name is **David Kizirian**, and I am a herpetologist at the American Museum of Natural History. A herpetologist studies animals such as snakes, lizards, frogs, and turtles. When I was three years old, I brought home a snake in a jar and presented it to my mother. I don't remember doing it, so I tell folks that I have been a herpetologist since before I can remember. I went to school for many years so I could get a job working at a museum, zoo, or university. I've been putting snakes in jars ever since!

The best part of my job is fieldwork, where I collect amphibians and reptiles in the wild. I especially like going to less-traveled parts of the world, like Ecuador, Mexico, Peru, and Vietnam, to look for new animal species. I have named more than 20 new species, including snakes, lizards, and even one frog. I am especially interested in studying microtelids, a group of rare lizards from the Andes Mountains in South America.

Part of my job involves taking care of the Museum's collection of amphibians and reptiles. The collection includes more than 350,000 specimens from all over the world. Occasionally, I work on exhibits and I teach, using the exhibition halls as classrooms. I also mentor students who might want to be scientists when they grow up—kids like you!